Alfabestiario

Poems
Antonello Borra

English Translations
Blossom S. Kirschenbaum

Art
Delia Robinson

Fomite
Burlington, Vermont

Poems Copyright © 2013 by Antonello Borra
Translations Copyright © 2013 Estate of Blossom S. Kirschenbaum
Art Copyright © 2013 by Delia Robinson

All rights reserved. No part of this book may be reproduced in any form or by any means without the prior written consent of the publisher, except in the case of brief quotations used in reviews and certain other noncommercial uses permitted by copyright law.

.

ISBN-13: 978-1-937677-41-1
Library of Congress Control Number: 2013932823

Fomite
58 Peru Street
Burlington, VT 05401
www.fomitepress.com

Cover Art - *Runner Ducks Walk Through a Mystery* - Delia Robinson
Author Photo - Clara Hösle

Alfabestiario

For Adriana (*la Schatza*)
and
For Blossom (*in memoriam*)

Contents

Acknowledgements i
Introduction by Roberto Piumini ii
L'albatro 2
The Albatross 3
L'anguilla 6
The Eel 7
L'aquila 10
The Eagle 11
La balena 14
The Whale 15
Il cane 18
The Dog 19
Il caprone 22
The Billy-Goat 23
La coccinella 26
The Ladybug 27
Il coniglio 30
The Rabbit 31
Il coccodrillo 34
The Crocodile 35
Il dodo 38
The Dodo 39
L'elefante 42
The Elephant 43
La faina 46
The Weasel 47
La folaga 50
The Moorhen 51
Il gallo 54
The Cock 55
Il gatto 58
The Cat 59
L'husky 62

The Husky	63
L'ippopotamo	66
The Hippopotamus	67
Lo jacaré	70
The Jacaré	71
Il kiwi	74
The Kiwi	75
La lepre	78
The Hare	79
Il lupo	82
The Wolf	83
Il maiale	86
The Pig	87
Il nibbio	90
The Kite	91
L'ornitorinco	94
The Platypus	95
La pantera	98
The Panther	99
La quaglia	102
The Quail	103
Il quetzal	106
The Quetzal	107
Il rospo	110
The Toad	111
Lo scarafaggio	114
The Cockroach	115
Il serpente	118
The Serpent	119
Il tacchino	122
The Turkey	123
La tartaruga	126
The Tortoise	127
Il topo	130
The Rat	131

Il toro 134
The Bull 135
L'upupa 138
The Hoopoe 139
La volpe 142
The Fox 143
Il wapiti 146
The Wapiti 147
Lo xenópodo 150
The Xenopous 151
Lo yak 154
The Yak 155
La zanzara 158
The Mosquito 159

Acknowledgements

These creatures closely resemble the ones gathered in *Alfabestiario* (Lietocolle: 2009), but are not exactly the same. Some new creatures joined in, others changed over the course of time. All of them celebrate the life and mourn the passing of Blossom S. Kirschenbaum, who had given them and their younger siblings from *Alphabetabestiario* (Fomite: 2011) a home in the English language. Their gratitude goes to many other humans: in the first place, Delia Robinson, for the drawings that accompany them here, and Roberto Piumini, for his words. To David (Dave) Cavanagh especially the creatures owe many a precious advice, as they do to Greg Delanty and Johannes Hösle.

They also would like to thank, in alphabetical order, Bren Alvarez, Giorgio Bàrberi Squarotti, Donna Bister, Michelangelo Camelliti, Marc Estrin, Luigi Fontanella, Valeria Gennero, Francesca Geymonat, Luisa Giacoma, Carla, Clara and Vittorio Hösle, Barbara Krohn, Niva Lorenzini, Gianni Martini, Anis Memon, Wolfgang Mieder, Sergio Parussa, Camillo Pennati, Emilio Rentocchini, Gino Ruozzi, Ricard Torrents, Carlo Alberto Sitta, Marco Vacchetti, Patrizia Valduga, and Paolo Valesio, who all know why.

In addition, some of these creatures peeked out of the pages of the following publications, whose editors they gratefully acknowledge: *In forma di parole*, *Literary Matters*, *Steve*, and *The WRUV Reader (A Vermont Writers' Anthology)*.

Introduction

It may in fact be that the entire animal kingdom – among its many intrinsic and worthy roles – acts as a "pet" to the entire human species. Like a sort of vast, limitless "band of companions" that we humans can hug tightly, or look in the eye for reassurance, relieving us of any burdensome personal otherness, and of all that risky, nerve-wracking emotional negotiation.

Once this condition has been established and poetically accepted, everything is fair game; and there are indeed many games in this collection of poems. There are some that we might call linguistic, as in the "Wapiti", which opens in a phonetic, descriptive vein, only to develop into a polished acrostic. There are games steeped in all of the world's timeless, ubiquitous carnivals, in which an animal mask sits on a human face in order to speak some painful or difficult truth.

In these poems, the animal mask of carnival rituals naturally, and with delicate severity, points to the face that lies beneath it, but there is also another recurring form of learned disguise at play: the proverbs, sayings and maxims that have always presented the animal universe as a human theater. The fox's advice is that "One has to be cunning in this world"; the wolf jests: "To shed one's hair and not lose one's natural vice, / that's what concerns me"; the cat slyly says: "Having nine lives like me / can allow one a spendthrift's luxury, / a couple of them given to dozing on divans". And so on.

This game would already be exquisitely enjoyable in itself, but the *Alfabestiario* does not stop at merely being ironic about the popular, fairytale element of animal masks; it does the same for philosophical, literary culture. Is "the cruelest month" for the turkey not November? After the cockroach warns that "it does no good to bolt the door / and bar the windows or set the alarm" against certain secret presences, it actually reinforces the Shakespearean couplet by prophesying: "You'll look at yourselves in the mirror one of these days / startled to see yourselves changed in certain ways."

Such sophistication could obviously have been a draw-back and a risk for this volume, with its refined complexity, its intent to please, its use of the linguistic and cultural *"trobar clus"*. Quite the contrary. The collection's complexity is clear and affectionate; it is never self-referential or showy.

The *Alfabestiario*'s excellence lies in its intertwining of culture (both anthropological and literary) and what I would call "fervent humanism", which leads to a quiet exhilaration that is sometimes melancholy but always light and bright.

This is indeed a very remarkable, "bright" work amidst the jumble of learned, statically speculative moanings that poetry so often serves up to us.

Not least of the book's merits is its emotional inspiration, the *"benedictio"*, which avoids being clouded or erased by metaphor and takes us back to the animal kingdom as such: to the vast community, the so-often mistreated companion in nature and existence that lives alongside us.

Roberto Piumini
Translated by Anis Memon

*... und die findigen Tiere merken es schon,
daß wir nicht sehr verläßlich zu Haus sind
in der gedeuteten Welt.*

R. M. Rilke

L'albatro

Far divertire un pubblico
non è roba da ridere,
soprattutto per me,
da cui ti aspetti, in genere,
qualche volo acrobatico,
qualche tuffo blasé
in azzurri simbolici.
So che rischio il ridicolo,
ma a me piace di più
il mestiere del comico,
benefico per l'anima
persino se sei tu
che piangi perché un perfido
ti trafigge lo stomaco e
diventi, lì per lì,
star di quanti impersonano
il ruolo della vittima.
Poi, comunque, si sa:
c'è sempre un che di tragico
nel destino di un comico.

The Albatross

To entertain the public
is no laughing matter.
Especially for me,
from whom you await, in general,
some sort of acrobatic flight,
some blasé plunge
into symbolic blue depths.
I know that I risk ridicule,
but I prefer
the craft of the comedian,
beneficial to the soul,
even if it's you
who cries because a sly wisecrack
strikes you in the gut and
you become, on the spot,
star among however many embody
the role of victim.
Well, anyway, as we know:
there's always a bit of the tragedian
in the destiny of a comedian.

L'anguilla

Mia sorella gemella
è molto intelligente,
ma è sempre stata pigra
e per questo è ingrassata.
Dice che non si sente
più bene e non ha voglia,
a quest'età, di farsi
un viaggio tanto lungo
per tornarsene indietro,
fin dove siamo nate
e per cosa? per mettere
al mondo qualche figlio,
che poi subito scappa
e finisce per fare
le stesse cose, errori
compresi, esattamente
come hai già fatto tu,
come hanno fatto i tuoi
e chissà mai quante altre
generazioni prima...

Forse ha ragione lei...
io comunque ho deciso
e parto anche da sola:
ho capito perché
detesto mia sorella.

The Eel

My twin sister
is very intelligent,
but she has always been lazy
and therefore has gotten fat.
She says she no longer feels
well and has no desire
at this age to undertake
an ever so long journey
just to go back
to where we were born
and what for? Bring forth
into the world some offspring
which then promptly absconds
and ends up by doing
the same things, mistakes
included, exactly as you
already have done,
and your folks have done
and who knows how many
generations way back have done...

Perhaps she is right...
I however have made up my mind
and I'm leaving even if I go alone:
I've come to understand why
I detest my sister.

L'aquila

Sarà per la mia vista non comune,
sarà che volo in alto più degli altri
e all'occasione scendo come il fulmine,
che mi si crede un uccello divino,
legame tra la terra e il cielo, simbolo
da chissà quanto della nobiltà
per cui non basta una preposizione.

Vi sorprende che rischio l'estinzione?

The Eagle

Maybe it's because of my uncommon eyesight,
maybe it's because I fly higher than the others
and sometimes plummet like lightning
that I am considered a bird divine,
a link between earth and heaven, a symbol
of nobility from who knows how far back
and so no preposition will suffice.

Does it surprise you that I risk extinction?

La balena

Io sono un mostro, un grande leviatano
dall'oscuro intestino che è un abisso.
Nella pancia mi è passato di tutto,
pure un profeta di nome Pinocchio,
che è tornato alla luce ad annunciare
ai tronchi d'albero che, un giorno, l'anima
del mondo avrebbe avuto la giustizia
che si attende da quando l'innocenza
si perde dando un morso ad una mela.

Capitani, più o meno coraggiosi,
senza sosta, da secoli mi danno
la caccia, caccia che è persecuzione:
fiocine, arpioni a squarciarmi la carne
per poi prendermi il grasso, farlo a pezzi,
bollirlo in pentoloni e farne l'olio.

A che vi serve l'olio? per le lampade?
a illuminarvi nelle vostre tenebre?

The Whale

I am a monster, a huge leviathan
with a dark intestine that is an abyss.
All and sundry have passed through my belly,
even a prophet by the name of Pinocchio,
who returned into daylight to announce
to the tree trunks that some day the soul
of the world would have the justice
it has awaited from the time when innocence
was lost by biting into an apple.

Captains more or less courageous
have for hundreds of years without rest
hunted me, their hunt a persecution;
hooks and harpoons to rend and rip my flesh
and then cut out my fat, chop it in pieces,
boil it in cauldrons to turn it to oil.

What use to you all is that oil? For your lamps?
To light up your tenebrous nights?

Il cane

Quando abbaio non dormo
e mordere non mordo
per il gusto di farlo,
semmai è per lavoro.
Non badate ai proverbi,
pensate alle parole.
E la parola cane,
per esempio, non morde.

The Dog

When I bark I don't sleep
and as for biting I don't bite
for the pleasure of doing so,
if I bite it's part of my job.
Pay no heed to the proverbs,
think about the words.
And the word dog,
for example, does not bite.

Il caprone

Ora... non voglio farne una tragedia,
la faccenda va avanti da millenni,
e sempre con lo stesso meccanismo:
vorrà dire qualcosa... In due parole:
vi raccontate che la colpa è mia
e tornate a sentirvi la coscienza
a posto. Dite: "Me l'ha fatto fare
il caprone, m'è apparso nella notte
del sabba del villaggio e la domenica
non sono andata a messa", per esempio,
o "Sentivo l'odore dello zolfo
poi è apparso il caprone e mi guardava,
ho perso i sensi e non ricordo più
niente di quello che è successo dopo".

Non è una mania di persecuzione,
però, a pensarci bene, queste corna
pesano e qualche conto non mi torna.

The Billy-Goat

Now... I don't want to make a tragedy out of it,
this kind of thing has been going on for millennia
and it always works the same way:
it may have its purpose... In short,
you tell yourselves that the fault is mine
and you go back feeling that your conscience
is clean. You say: "What made me do it is
the billy-goat, he appeared to me in the night,
Saturday night in the village and on Sunday
I did not go to Mass," for instance,
or "I smelled the odor of sulphur and
then the billy-goat appeared, was staring at me,
I fainted dead away and recall nothing
of what happened afterwards."

It's not a zeal for persecution;
however, on due consideration these horns
weigh heavily and a certain bill remains unpaid.

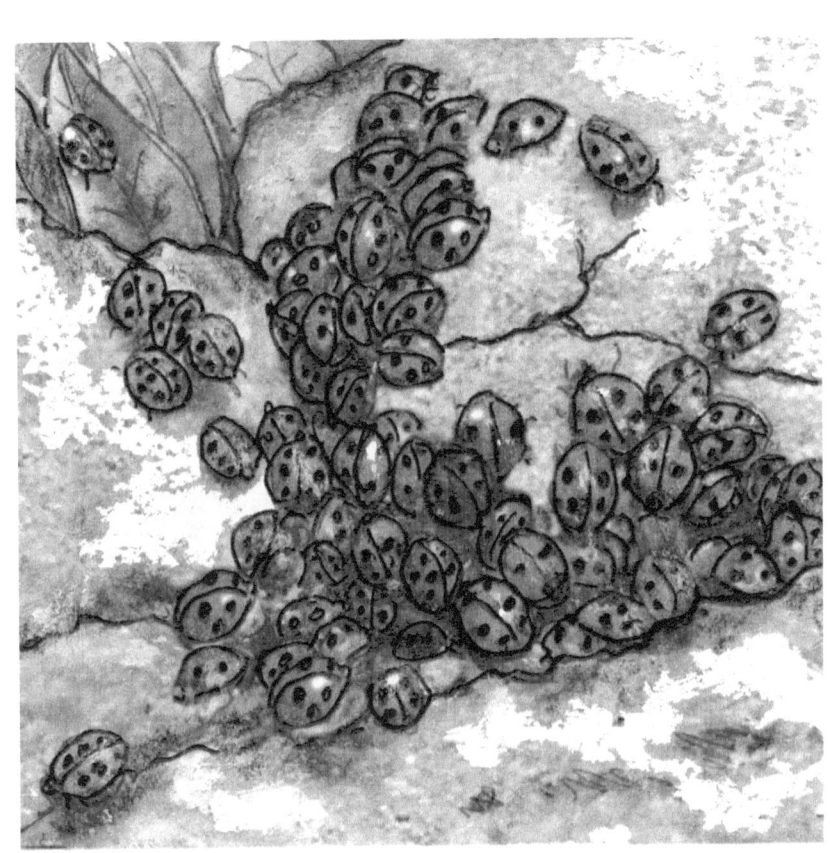

La coccinella

Noi coccinelle portiamo fortuna
e trovarvene in casa cinquecento
dovrebbe farvi sentir fortunati
oltre ogni aspettativa: sì. Purtroppo,
la mancanza di misura spaventa e
non porta fortuna a noi coccinelle.

The Ladybug

We ladybugs bring good luck
and to find in your home five hundred of us
should make you people feel lucky
beyond every expectation: yes. Unfortunately,
the immoderation terrifies, and
does not bring good luck to us ladybugs.

Il coniglio

Ma cos'avrà poi tanto
da correre e saltare
mia cugina, la lepre?
In pentola finisce
pure lei, prima o poi.
Magari le va peggio
e se la sbrana ancora
viva qualche altra bestia.
E che vita è mai quella,
sempre all'aperto, al freddo,
al caldo, alle intemperie,
se si sta tanto bene
qui dentro tutti insieme!
Cosa c'è di più bello
di una famiglia unita?

The Rabbit

But whatever got into her
to set her running and jumping like that,
my cousin the hare?
She'll end up in the skillet
sooner or later, even she.
Or it could go still worse for her
were some other wild beast to rip
her to pieces alive.
And what kind of life does she have
always out in the open, in the cold,
in the heat, in rain and storm,
when we're so much better off
here inside all together!
What is more lovely
than a united family?

Il coccodrillo

Quante lacrime ho sparso in vita mia!
ma è una questione di fisiologia:
rimordono i miei denti, la coscienza
no. Tormenti di quel tipo li lascio
ad anime più belle, ma con scarpe
di pelle, pelle un po' come la mia.

The Crocodile

How many tears I have shed in my life!
But it's a matter of physiology:
my teeth lacerate, my conscience
does not. Torments of that type I leave
to souls more refined but with shoes of leather,
leather that somewhat reminds of my skin.

Il dodo

Voi pensate soltanto ai dinosauri,
così dite che non è colpa vostra...
Ma il tilacino, il quagga, l'alca, l'uro,
il visone marino, l'aepyornis,
il delfino dello Yangtze, l'antilope
azzurra, i moa, il gufo facciabianca
e tutti quelli di cui resta solo
un'eco, un nome, un osso, dei disegni
in un museo com'è successo a me?
Ve lo dico in parole molto semplici:
state attenti: prima o poi, tocca a voi.

The Dodo

You think only about the dinosaurs,
thus you say that it is not your fault...
but what of the Tasmanian tiger, the plains zebra,
the auk, the auroch, the sea mink, the elephant bird,
the Yangtze river dolphin, the blue
antelope, the wingless moa, the white-faced owl
and all those of whom there remains only
an echo, a name, a bone, some drawings
in a museum as is the case with me?
I tell you in very simple words:
take care: sooner or later, it's your turn.

L'elefante

Pensando a quel negozio di cristalli
dove, chissà perché, sarei entrato,
mi ricordo di questi insegnamenti:
beati quelli con poca memoria,
il dolore rimargina e non lascia
cicatrici; beati quelli a cui
mancano le zanne, con la bruttezza
non s'induce nessuno in tentazione;
beati i piccoli, purché non nani,
sembrano avere davanti un futuro;
beati quelli nati dentro a un circo,
la loro ricompensa sa di zucchero,
la catena alla zampa tiene a casa;
beati quelli che, senza vederla,
crederanno alla savana; beati
quanti cercano quel che non esiste,
perché di loro è il nostro cimitero.

The Elephant

Thinking about the china shop
where who knows why I had gone in,
I remember those schoolroom instructions:
blessed are those with poor memory,
their grief will heal and not leave any
scars; blessed are those who lack tusks
or teeth to flaunt, ugliness never
seduced anyone into temptation;
blessed the little ones, if only they're not dwarfs,
for they seem to have a future before them;
blessed those born into a circus,
their recompense will taste of sugar,
the chain around their hoof binds them to home;
blessed those who without seeing it
believe in the savannah; blessed
all those who seek what does not exist,
because theirs is our elephants' cemetery.

La faina

Non sono scaltra, avida o maligna,
certo non più di quelle che mi vogliono
per farsi una pelliccia con la mia,
e con la scusa che sono una ladra.
Sarà, ma sono una ladra di polli...

E che razza di giustizia è la vostra,
ammazzarmi per poi mettervi in mostra?

The Weasel

I am not crafty, greedy or malicious,
surely not more than those who chase after me
wanting to make their fur coat out of mine
and with the excuse that I am a thief.
Maybe so, but I'm a thief of chickens...

And to what brand of justice have you aspired,
to kill me and then show yourselves off to be admired?

La folaga

Tutti i problemi dell'identità,
per me, non sono che un battito d'ali:
quello di una qualunque mia compagna
di volo, a me perfettamente analoga.

The Moorhen

All the problems about identity
are for me just a flapping of wings:
the stroke of any companion who flies
with me, perfectly equivalent to me.

Il gallo

In quell'attimo incerto,
che ancora non è giorno
ma neppure è più notte,
sta tutto il mio sapere.

Per questo non c'è femmina
che mi possa resistere.

The Cock

In that uncertain moment
which is not yet day
but neither any longer night
is poised all my knowing.

Consequently, no female
can resist me.

Il gatto

Avendo sette vite come me,
puoi permetterti il lusso di sprecarne
un paio a dormicchiare sui divani,
a stiracchiarti a piacimento, a fare
le fusa a chi di vita ne ha una sola,
a giocare con il topo del tempo
sapendo che poi vince sempre lui.

E infatti l'ultima vita è difficile,
quando sto in giro per tutta la notte
a lamentarmi che sembro un bambino,
oppure a trasformarmi in donna adulta
che sa il senso delle cose e ne soffre
e si circonda di gatti randagi,
che non sono né buoni né malvagi.

The Cat

Having nine lives like me
can allow one a spendthrift's luxury,
a couple of them given to dozing on divans,
stretched out voluptuously, purring
to those whose lives are limited only to one,
playing with the mouse of time knowing
that in the end the winner will always be him.

Yet in fact the final life is difficult,
when I'm making my rounds through the night
lamenting so that I sound like a child
or else to transform into a mature woman
who knows and suffers the meaning of things
and is surrounded by strays such as you find,
street cats who are neither wicked nor kind.

L'husky

A qualcuno è il colore
degli occhi, quel che resta
del freddo nelle notti
lunghe un inverno intero,
che comunque era casa.
A voi resta che cosa?
nostalgie di una stella
polare? di una slitta,
o quant'altro, che porta
in esilio? la luce
di un ricordo appassito:
quell'impressione acuta,
e comunque infondata,
di meritare il cielo?

The Husky

For someone it's the color
of the eyes, what remains
of the chill through nights
long as an entire winter,
which however was home.
And for you there, what remains?
Longings for a star, the North
Star? Perhaps for a sled,
or some other thing that took you
into exile? The light
of a withered memory:
that keen impression,
however groundless and vain,
of deserving heaven?

L'ippopotamo

E se ci fosse un posto
per me su in paradiso?
Pensate un po' che scherzo,
soprattutto per quelli
che, abituati a vedermi
sempre sporco di fango,
vedono in me la bestia,
nient'altro che la bestia.
Dio non mi sembra il tipo
che bada alle apparenze...

Beh? e mo' tutti a bocca
aperta inorriditi?
che ho fatto, bestemmiato?

The Hippopotamus

And if there were a place
for me up in paradise?
Think what a good joke,
above all for those
who, accustomed to seeing me
always filthy with mud,
see me as the beast,
nothing other than the beast.
To me God doesn't seem the type
to bother about appearances.

Now what? All agape
simply horrified?
What've I done, blasphemed?

Lo jacaré

Senza star troppo a farla
lunga, in un'altra lingua,
ad altre latitudini,
non sono che un caimano
con il muso più largo
e le stesse abitudini.

The Jacaré

Without stretching out a long
story in another tongue,
in other latitudes,
I am only a cayman,
with snout a bit broader,
and the same habitudes.

Il kiwi

Siete killer da sempre,
io roba da kebab,
krapfen di carne, pollo
senz'ali kaputt subito.
E se ci fosse un karma?

The Kiwi

You guys are killers since forever,
I'm stuff for kebab,
crullers of meat, wingless chicken
promptly kaput.
And if there were a karma?

La lepre

Prendete mio cugino, per esempio:
pavido, smidollato, chiuso in gabbia
a fare figli per fare stufati.
Io sono agile, scattante, veloce,
sempre all'aperto, libera, selvatica,
e prima di finire nella pentola
faccio in modo che venga l'appetito.
Da me prende il suo nome il levriero,
da mio cugino viene 'conigliera'.
Chi lo direbbe che siamo parenti?

The Hare

Take my cousin, for example:
timid, caged, no marrow to the bones,
breeding more rabbits to be cooked into stews.
I'm nimble, quick-hopping, fast,
always outdoors, free, in the wild,
and before I end in the casserole
I'll make sure a chase whets your appetite.
From me, "*lepre*," comes the greyhound's name "*levriero*,"
from my cousin comes "conigliera," "rabbit warren,"
who would guess we're related?

Il lupo

Perdere il pelo e non perdere il vizio,
questo mi tocca. E chi vuol farsi agnello
è avvertito, si chiami Caio o Tizio:
se ho fame, non importa questo o quello.

The Wolf

To shed one's hair and not lose one's natural vice,
that's what concerns me. And whoever wants to play sheep
is warned, whether Tom, Dick or Harry, however nice:
if I'm hungry it makes no difference on whom I'll leap.

Il maiale

Problemi con il corpo?
ad accettare il fatto
che prima o poi tradisce,
abbandona e ritorna
da sua madre, la terra?

Io di certi problemi
non so che cosa farmene:
porto il nome di mamma,
conosco il mio destino
e per questo non faccio
tante storie per vitto,
alloggio e pulizia:
bivacco nel momento
pure se sa di merda.
Non mi offendo di certo
se mi chiamate porco.

The Pig

Doubts about the body?
About accepting the fact
that sooner or later it betrays,
abandons, and goes back
to its mother, the earth?

As for me I don't know
what to make of such doubts:
I carry the name of my mother,
know my destiny
and on this score do not raise
such a fuss over room,
board, and hygiene.
I spend the night where night falls,
even if it smells of dung.
Be sure I take no offense
if you call me swine.

Il nibbio

Sono di quelli che strappano teste
senza stare a far tanti complimenti.
Sono fatto così: scendo dall'alto,
tutto d'un tratto, a ammazzare chi voglio
e non vedo problemi, se sta bene
al dio che mi ha creato questi artigli,
che al dolore dei più sembra sbadigli.

The Kite

I'm among those who tear off heads
without so much as a by-your-leave.
I'm made that way: I swoop from on high
all of a sudden to kill as I please
and I see no problems, as long as it suits
the God who created these claws for me,
who seems to yawn at the pain of most creatures.

L'ornitorinco

Eccomi qui a nuotare
a occhi chiusi, in sostanza
un piedipiatti all'angolo
di un incrocio arbitrario.
Confondervi le idee,
o le categorie,
questo è il mio imperativo.
Con il becco ho poppato
al ventre del divino:
il cosmo è meno rigido
di quanto voi pensiate.

The Platypus

Look at me swimming here
with eyes shut, substantially
a flat-footed body at the corner
of an arbitrary intersection.
To confuse your ideas,
or your categories,
this is my responsibility.
With my bill I have suckled
at the bosom of the divine:
the cosmos is less hard and fast
than you might think.

La pantera

E chi lo sente più
questo profumo dolce
che spando attorno a me,
bestia tra le altre bestie
rinchiuse nello zoo?

Ormai guardo nel vuoto,
anche una volontà
più forte della mia
si piegherebbe a queste
sbarre. Ed io sono stanca
di andare avanti e indietro
e di girare in tondo
coi miei passi felpati,
come se un mondo fuori
esistesse davvero.

Quel tanto di divino
che discende da me
potrebbe, forse, ancora
riscattare ogni vostro
peccato. Sì, peccato...

The Panther

And who smells anymore
this sweet perfume
that I spread around me,
beast among the other beasts
locked up in the zoo?

By now I look into the void,
even volition
stronger than mine
would fold in defeat at these
bars and I am weary
of pacing to and fro, to and fro,
turning in circles
pacing on velvet paws
as if a further world beyond
might really exist.

That touch of the divine
that emanates from me
perhaps could even yet
redeem your every
sin. Yes, sin...

La quaglia

Quel quid che manca al qui
ed ora, quel quesito
o quel quanto di luce
querula che non quadra
con quote e con questioni,
coi quiz del quotidiano
è una quieta quisquilia
un quid pro quo banale
quanto un salto da quaglia.

The Quail

That much that's quite missing
in the here and now, that question
or that quantum of
querulous light not making sense
with the quotas, the queries
and the daily quizzes
is a quiet trifle,
a quid pro quo as banal
as the leap of a quail.

Il quetzal

Come va in Guatemala?!
Va come va in qualunque
altro luogo, in qualunque
altro tempo del sacro:
le tue piume a qualcuno,
le tue carni ad un altro.

The Quetzal

How it goes in Guatemala?!
It goes as it goes in any
other place, in any
other time of the sacred:
your feathers to some,
your flesh to some other.

Il rospo

Sono un rospo, prosaico
in questa mia bruttezza
che da sola sarebbe
condanna sufficiente
senza anche i pregiudizi
e le persecuzioni.

Concorderete tutti:
non è bello esser brutti.

The Toad

I am a toad, prosaic
in this my ugliness
that in itself would be
punishment enough
without also the prejudices
and the persecutions.

You will surely all agree:
it's not lovely to be ugly.

Lo scarafaggio

Sono l'insetto scuro che trovate
nella vasca da bagno, oppure dentro
al vostro lavandino, se per caso
accendete la luce quando è notte
fonda intorno. Capite in quell'istante
che non siete al sicuro in casa vostra,
che i muri, i pavimenti, ed il soffitto
sono pieni di passaggi segreti e
non serve a niente sprangare le porte
e le finestre e mettere l'allarme.

Un giorno vi guarderete allo specchio,
vi parrà di esser cambiati parecchio.

The Cockroach

I'm the dark insect that you find
in the bathtub or inside
your porcelain sink, if by chance
you turn on the light in the middle of
the night. At once you grasp
that you're not so safe and sound in your own home,
that the walls, the floors, and the ceiling
are full of secret passages and
it does no good to bolt the door
and bar the windows or set the alarm.

You'll look at yourselves in the mirror one of these days
startled to see yourselves changed in certain ways.

Il serpente

...e da che il mondo è mondo, se la prendono
con me, come se fosse colpa mia
che la donna è curiosa e credulona
e l'uomo poi fa quello che lei vuole.
Ma quale bestia immonda e tentatrice!?
non è un laccio per tendere tranelli
il cerchio che disegno se mi mordo
la coda e il mio principio si congiunge,
nascondendola forse, con la fine...

The Serpent

...and since the world began they go on blaming
me as if it were some fault of mine
that woman is curious and credulous
and man does whatever she asks of him.
How dare they call me dirty tempting beast!?
That's no string to tighten a trap,
the circle that I form if I bite my tail
and my beginning unites with it,
hiding my end, perhaps...

Il tacchino

Per me è novembre il mese più crudele,
quando i più pensano di render grazie
a dio con un massacro di tacchini,
in questo mondo niente affatto nuovo.
Pertanto anch'io, dovendo render grazie,
rendo grazie per chi non mangia carne.

The Turkey

To me the cruelest month is November,
when most folks think about giving thanks
to God with a massacre of turkeys
in this world that's hardly new.
Therefore, I too, if obliged to give thanks,
give thanks for those who don't eat meat.

La tartaruga

La pazienza s'impara,
basta vivere a lungo e
prendersela con calma,
ché più di un piè veloce
s'è già perso per strada,
ben prima del traguardo,
o ha dovuto fermarsi
per male ad un garretto.

E la bellezza conta
e non conta, guardatemi:
ruga più, ruga meno,
bella non sono stata
mai, neppure da giovane,
ma sono ancora qui
a sfidare l'idea
che il tempo è un assassino.

Porto il peso del mondo
intero sul mio dorso,
non giratemi a zampe
in su, non vi conviene,
anche se questo guscio,
senza funzioni ermetiche,
non vale più una lira ed
è una casa da zingari.

The Tortoise

One learns to be patient.
It's enough to live long
and calmly take everything in stride,
since more than one fleet of foot
has already collapsed along the way
well before the finish-line
or has had to quit
because of a sprained ankle.

And beauty both does
and does not count, look at me:
a wrinkle more, a wrinkle less,
good-looking I never was
not even in my younger days,
but I'm still here
to challenge the idea
that time is an assassin.

I carry the weight of the entire
world on my back.
Don't turn me upside down.
That doesn't befit you
even if this shell,
lacking hermetic functions,
is hardly worth a cent and
is a home fit only for gypsies.

Il topo

Figlio della montagna
delle vostre paure
sono un ingenuo anch'io.
Quando ancora ero piccolo,
ho visto un pipistrello
e ho pensato che fosse
un angelo del cielo,
che annunciava imminente
l'agognata scomparsa
di tutti i pifferai
che ci vogliono male.

Quando potremo vivere
dove e come vogliamo,
senza dovere sempre
fare la stessa fine?

The Rat

Son of the mountain
of your fears
I too am an innocent.
When I was still small
I saw a bat
and I thought it was
a heaven-sent angel
announcing the imminent
eagerly awaited vanishing
of all the pied pipers
that intend our destruction.

When will we ever be able to live
where and how we please,
not obliged always
to meet the same old end?

Il toro

"In principio è l'immagine del toro",
inizia il mio vangelo di corride
e sacrifici fatti a questo e a quello,
alfabeto del sangue dell'Europa,
di serenate a Venere e alla luna,
di figli mostri solo per metà,
di concorrenza a quelli della croce...

Se parlo per enigmi è perché almeno
la mia sensualità non è un mistero.

The Bull

"In the beginning is the image of the bull,"
so starts my gospel of the bull-fighting ritual
and sacrifices made to the glory of this or that,
an alphabet of Europe's blood,
of serenades to Venus and the moon,
of offspring monsters by only half,
of competing with followers of the cross…

If I speak through riddles it's because at least
my lust is no mystery.

L'upupa

Se il mio nome fa il verso alle mie voci,
io faccio la mia cresta sulla vostra
spesa inutile: spreco di parole.
Se ne dicono tante sul mio conto:
per uno sono ilare, per un altro
tutto l'opposto. Ma come lo sanno?!
Mi ritagliano addosso i loro panni
sporchi di questioni letterarie:
c'è chi intinge la sua penna nel mio sangue
per scrivere incantesimi e chi cerca
tra i miei versi un suo tesoro smarrito.

Io continuo a ripetere la stessa
cosa: non qui, più in là, più in là, più in là.

The Hoopoe

If my name seems to mock my calls,
I make my crest atop your useless
expenditure, a waste of words.
Many different things are said about me:
one is that I'm hilarious, and another
just the opposite. But how would they know?!
They cut the dirty shirts off their backs
carrying on with literary questions:
there's one who dips his pen in my blood
to write magic spells and another who seeks
among my verses a lost treasure of his own.

I continue to repeat the same
thing: not here but up, up above, up above, up above.

La volpe

Bisogna farsi furbi, a questo mondo:
chi si fa agnello il lupo se lo mangia,
tanto per fare il nome di un parente
senza tutti gli scrupoli che ho io.
Se non sei tu che badi ai tuoi affari,
chi vuoi mai che lo faccia? e non è il caso
di essere squali o di essere sciacalli,
basta quel po' d'astuzia, intelligenza
obliqua, aguzza come questi denti.

Devi saper parlare con la gente,
capire come tira il vento e fare
presto a prendere l'occasione al volo,
se non la prendi tu, la prende un altro:
grazie al cielo, non mancano gli allocchi
e quelli col cervello da gallina.
Poi, tanto per capirci, essere femmina
non è facile, in questo porco mondo.

Ma cosa vi credete? che sia tutto
essere sexy, rosse e impellicciate?

The Fox

One has to be cunning in this world:
who plays the sheep will be eaten by the wolf,
just to mention a relative of mine
lacking in all the scruples that I maintain.
If you don't care for your own business
who do you expect to do it for you? It's not a matter of
being sharks, or of being jackals,
what's enough is a bit of craftiness, oblique
intelligence and sharpness like these teeth.

You have to know how to speak to people,
to understand which way the wind blows, and seize
the opportunity promptly to hit and run.
If you don't, somebody else will take it.
Thank heaven there's no shortage of nincompoops
and those with the brains of a clucking hen.
Besides, as we well know, being female
is not easy in this dirty world.

But what do you folks believe? That all it takes
is being sexy, rosy and wearing furs?

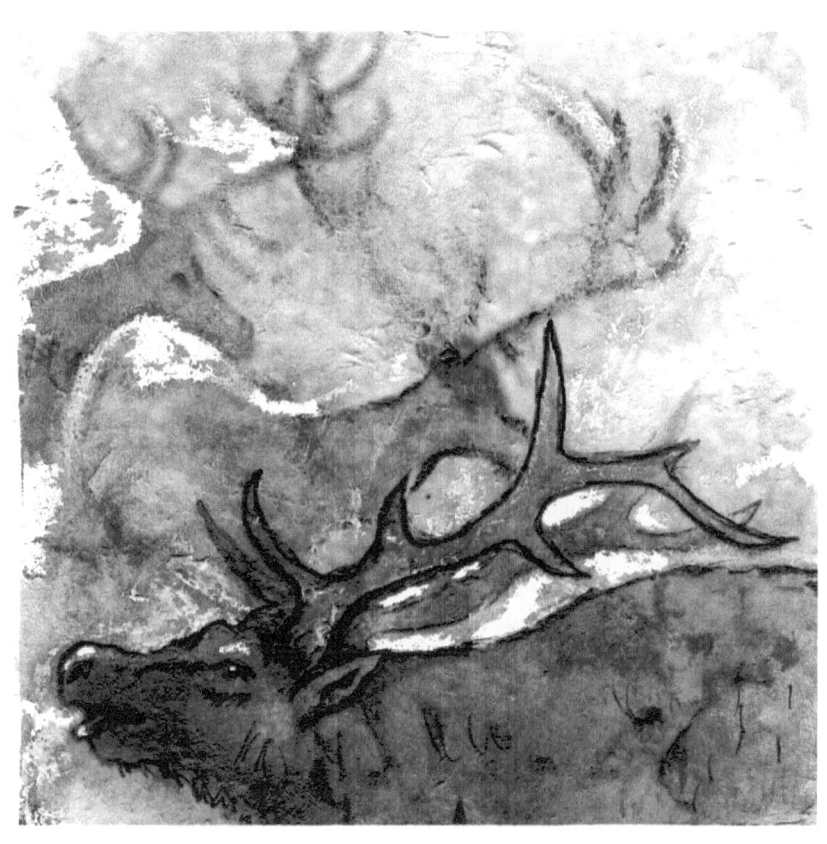

Il wapiti

Wapiti wapiti wapiti wa...

Come l'eco nel sogno di un galoppo,
e certamente è qualcuno che scappa;
rumino spesso di scappare anch'io,
vivere altrove, lontano dal branco,
ovunque, ma non qui e con queste corna.

C'è un mio ritratto in caverne antichissime,
anche questo è durare, ma non basta,
non è la sopravvivenza da specie
a stare a cuore a ciascun individuo;
dovrà ben esserci qualche risposta
e non solo con l'anima. A proposito,
sono sempre più assillato da un dubbio:
esser vegetariani acquista l'anima

a un animale come il soprascritto?

The Wapiti

Wapiti wapiti wapiti wa...

Like the echo in the dream of a gallop,
and surely it is someone escaping;
often chewing my cud I too ponder escape,
to live elsewhere, far from the herd,
anywhere but not here, not with these horns.

There's my portrait in a prehistoric cave;
this too means to last, but it doesn't suffice,
it's not the survival of the species
that's of prime concern to the individual heart;
some greater response is called for, and
not only with the soul. By the way,
I'm more and more beset by a misgiving:
does being vegetarian reward with a soul
an animal like yours truly?

Lo xenópodo

Non ho poi molto per farmi notare,
nonostante il mio nome, le mie zampe
e la mia doppia vita senza code
(se così si può dire del processo
per cui passo dalla tassidermia
a riempitivo per tassonomie).

The Xenopous

Not really much to make me conspicuous,
despite my name, my paws,
and my double life without tails
(or so one might refer to the process
by which I pass from taxidermy
to expletive for taxonomies.)

Lo yak

Sono il bue tibetano,
se guardo verso l'alto
vedo bene che il cielo
mi sta tanto vicino
che quasi lo potrei
sfiorare con le corna.
Poi ricordo che il saggio
china il capo e contempla
anche quanto sta in basso.

The Yak

I am the ox from Tibet.
If I ever look up
I see well that the sky
is so close to me
I could almost
graze it with my horns.
Then I reflect that the wise
bow their heads and revere
also what lies below.

La zanzara

Spegni la luce. Incomincio a ronzare.
Speri d'aver sentito male, provi
a far finta di niente e io continuo.
Riaccendi e tutto ritorna tranquillo,
tu no, perché sai che tanto ti pungo
e cominci a grattarti senza posa.
Tanto è il fastidio della mia presenza,
che finisci per prenderti anche a schiaffi
da solo, pur di farmi stare zitta.
Chi sono? la tua cattiva coscienza?

The Mosquito

You turn out the light. I start to hum.
You hope you've not heard right; you try
to pretend it's nothing and I keep humming.
You turn the light back on and again all is calm,
except you, because you know that anyhow I'll bite
and you will start to scratch without repose.
Such is the needling of my presence
that you're driven to slapping at
your own self trying to silence me.
What am I? Your pricking conscience?

Antonello Borra - Poems

Antonello Borra teaches Italian at the University of Vermont. His other volumes of poetry are *Frammenti di tormenti (prima parte)* (Longo: 2000), *Frammenti di tormenti (seconda parte)* (Lietocolle: 2006), *Alfabestiario* (Lietocolle: 2009), and the illustrated, bilingual *Alphabetabestiario* (Fomite: 2011). The texts presented here are not exactly the same published in Italy in 2009. Translations of his poetry appeared in English, Catalan, and are being prepared in German. He translated into Italian poems from the English of Greg Delanty, W.S. Merwin, and Gerry Murphy; from the German of Erich Fried; from the Spanish of Tina Escaja, Roberto Sosa, and José Watanabe. He co-translated two autobiographical novels from the German of Johannes Hösle and is a regular contributor to magazines and journals in both Italy and the United States. His other publications are books and articles on literary criticism and language pedagogy.

Blossom S. Kirschenbaum (1933-2011) - Translations

Member of PEN (New York Center), the American Italian Historical Association, and the Modern Language Association, Blossom S. Kirschenbaum, a "Hunter Girl" from grades 7 through 12, took her B.A. at Hunter College, her M.A. (1972) and Ph.D. (1976) from Brown University. She contributed to encyclopedias and sourcebooks, published scholarly articles in Italian-American and Jewish-American journals; and wrote an Afterword to Ginevra Bompiani's *L'Orso maggiore (The Great Bear)*. Translations from Italian include poems (*Fables from Trastevere*, from the Roman poet known as Trilussa, 1976); novels (Giuliana Morandini's *I cristalli di Vienna*, as *Bloodstains*, 1987; Paola Drigo's Maria *Zef*, 1989) and stories (two by Marina Mizzau are featured in *New Italian Women*, now in its 4th paperback printing). Stefano Benni's "Sigismondo and Vittorina" in her translation took the lead in Chelsea 66 (1999) and his "Una rosa rossa" as "One Red Rose," appeared bilingually in the *Journal of Italian Translation*, II:2, Fall 2008). "Augusto Romano, Italian Modernist" in her translation was the cover article for *Modernism* (12:4, Winter 2009-10).

I came to the Alfabestiario without prior plan. Antonello sent me, via e-mail, poems from the original collection published in Italy. I loved them, and began to translate as a way of sharing my enthusiasm with friends who don't read Italian—but obsession soon took over, I got entangled in the toils and joys of translation itself, and in discussions of poetic contexts, and in the history of the "bestiary", a genre popular in the European Middle Ages describing—and often moralizing—various real or mythical kinds of animals, but reaching back to fabulous beasts and monsters of Greek mythology and with contemporary examples continuing to emerge.

Delia Robinson - Art

I grew up in a divided world. Part of the year I lived in my father's household where intellect was king. Einstein lived across the street in a neighborhood strewn with Nobel Laureates. These old world scholars discussed Plato around our dinner table, great men all, transformed by genius into half-gods. Where were the great women? Maybe there weren't any. Females were ornamental, expected to flatter and charm, useful for biological or culinary abilities.

The rest of the year I lived an intensely rural life in Southern Indiana. My grade school had a ten-hole outhouse, water was served in a dipper from a galvanized bucket, and books were delivered by library truck. Our household matriarchy was colored by dream, imagination, and song. Who told the best stories? Where was the best blackberry patch? What birds were nesting in the wisteria vine? We laughed, sang, picked beans, read, sewed, drew, and squabbled. Women were reliable but men came and went, valued primarily for their strength, biological functions, and money making skills.

Perhaps this explains my take on the world as reflected in art. My view is bioptic, cross-eyed, fragmented, salty, bitter, yet still hopeful. My work is overloaded with information, stories, color, and images—most original, some pilfered, some in transition.

Fomite
Burlington, Vermont

Fomite is a literary press whose authors and artists explore the human condition—political, cultural, personal and historical—in poetry and prose.

A fomite is a medium capable of transmitting infectious organisms from one individual to another.

"The activity of art is based on the capacity of people to be infected by the feelings of others." Tolstoy, *What is Art?*

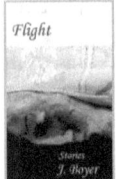

Flight and Other Stories - Jay Boyer
In *Flight and Other Stories,* we're with the fattest woman on earth as she draws her last breaths and her soul ascends toward its final reward. We meet a divorcee who can fly for no more effort than flapping her arms. We follow a middle-aged butler whose love affair with a young woman leads him first to the mysteries of bondage, and then to the pleasures of malice. Story by story, we set foot into worlds so strange as to seem all but surreal, yet everything feels familiar, each moment rings true. And that's when we recognize we're in the hands of one of America's truly original talents.

Loisaida - Dan Chodorokoff
Catherine, a young anarchist estranged from her parents and squatting in an abandoned building on New York's Lower East Side is fighting with her boyfriend and conflicted about her work on an underground newspaper. After learning of a developer's plans to demolish a community garden, Catherine builds an alliance with a group of Puerto Rican community activists. Together they confront the confluence of politics, money, and real estate that rule Manhattan. All the while she learns important lessons from her great-grandmother's life in the Yiddish anarchist movement that flourished on the Lower East Side at the turn of the century. In this coming of age story, family saga, and tale of urban politics, Dan Chodorkoff explores the "principle of hope", and examines how memory and imagination inform social change.

Improvisational Arguments - Anna Faktorovich
Improvisational Arguments is written in free verse to capture the essence of modern problems and triumphs. The poems clearly relate short, frequently humorous and occasionally tragic, stories about travels to exotic and unusual places, fantastic realms, abnormal jobs, artistic innovations, political objections, and misadventures with love.

Loosestrife - Greg Delanty
This book is a chronicle of complicity in our modern lives, a witnessing of war and the destruction of our planet. It is also an attempt to adjust the more destructive blueprint myths of our society. Often our cultural memory tells us to keep quiet about the aspects that are most challenging to our ethics, to forget the violations we feel and tremors that keep us distant and numb.

Fomite
Burlington, Vermont

Carts and Other Stories - Zdravka Evtimova

Roots and wings are the key words that best describe the short story collection, *Carts and Other Stories,* by Zdravka Evtimova. The book is emotionally multilayered and memorable because of its internal power, vitality and ability to touch both the heart and your mind. Within its pages, the reader discovers new perspectives and true wealth, and learns to see the world with different eyes. The collection lives on the borders of different cultures. *Carts and Other Stories* will take the reader to wild and powerful Bulgarian mountains, to silver rains in Brussels, to German quiet winter streets and to wind bitten crags in Afghanistan. This book lives for those seeking to discover the beauty of the world around them, and will have them appreciating what they have—and perhaps what they have lost as well.

The Listener Aspires to the Condition of Music - Barry Goldensohn

"I know of no other selected poems that selects on one theme, but this one does, charting Goldensohn's career-long attraction to music's performance, consolations and its august, thrilling, scary and clownish charms. Does all art aspire to the condition of music as Pater claimed, exhaling in a swoon toward that one class act? Goldensohn is more aware than the late 19th century of the overtones of such breathing: his poems thoroughly round out those overtones in a poet's lifetime of listening."
John Peck, poet, editor, Fellow of the American Academy of Rome

The Co-Conspirator's Tale - Ron Jacobs

There's a place where love and mistrust are never at peace; where duplicity and deceit are the universal currency. *The Co-Conspirator's Tale* takes place within this nebulous firmament. There are crimes committed by the police in the name of the law. Excess in the name of revolution. The combination leaves death in its wake and the survivors struggling to find justice in a San Francisco Bay Area noir by the author of the underground classic *The Way the Wind Blew: A History of the Weather Underground* and the novel *Short Order Frame Up*.

When You Remember Deir Yassin - R.L. Green

When You Remember Deir Yassin is a collection of poems by R. L. Green, an American Jewish writer, on the subject of the occupation and destruction of Palestine. Green comments: "Outspoken Jewish critics of Israeli crimes against humanity have, strangely, been called 'anti-Semitic' as well as the hilariously illogical epithet 'self-hating Jews.' As a Jewish critic of the Israeli government, I have come to accept these accusations as a stamp of approval and a badge of honor, signifying my own fealty to a central element of Jewish identity and ethics: one must be a lover of truth and a friend to the oppressed, and stand with the victims of tyranny, not with the tyrants, despite tribal loyalty or self-advancement. These poems were written as expressions of outrage, and of grief, and to encourage my sisters and brothers of every cultural or national grouping to speak out against injustice, to try to save Palestine, and in so doing, to reclaim for myself my own place as part of the Jewish people." Poems in the original English are accompanied by Arabic and Hebrew translations.

Fomite
Burlington, Vermont

Roadworthy Creature, Roadworthy Craft - Kate Magill

Words fail but the voice struggles on. The culmination of a decade's worth of performance poetry, *Roadworthy Creature, Roadworthy Craft* is Kate Magill's first full-length publication. In lines that are sinewy yet delicate, Magill's poems explore the terrain where idea and action meet, where bodies and words commingle to form a strange new flesh, a breathing text, an "I" that spirals outward from itself.

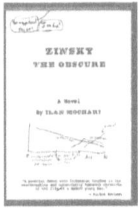

Zinsky the Obscure - Ilan Mochari

"If your childhood is brutal, your adulthood becomes a daily attempt to recover: a quest for ecstasy and stability in recompense for their early absence." So states the 30-year-old Ariel Zinsky, whose bachelor-like lifestyle belies the torturous youth he is still coming to grips with. As a boy, he struggles with the beatings themselves; as a grownup, he struggles with the world's indifference to them. *Zinsky the Obscure* is his life story, a humorous chronicle of his search for a redemptive ecstasy through sex, an entrepreneurial sports obsession, and finally, the cathartic exercise of writing it all down. Fervently recounting both the comic delights and the frightening horrors of a life in which he feels —always—that he is not like all the rest, Zinsky survives the worst and relishes the best with idiosyncratic style, as his heartbreak turns into self-awareness and his suicidal ideation into self-regard. A vivid evocation of the all-consuming nature of lust and ambition —and the forces that drive them.

The Derivation of Cowboys & Indians - Joseph D. Reich

The Derivation of Cowboys & Indians represents a profound journey, a breakdown of The American Dream from a social, cultural, historical, and spiritual point of view. Reich examines in concise detail the loss of the collective unconscious, commenting on our contemporary postmodern culture with its self-interested excesses, on where and how things all go wrong, and how social/political practice rarely meets its original proclamations and promises. Reich's surreal and self-effacing satire brings this troubling message home. *The Derivations of Cowboys & Indians* is a desperate search and struggle for America's literal, symbolic, and spiritual home.

Visiting Hours - Jennifer Anne Moses

Visiting Hours, a novel-in-stories, explores the lives of people not normally met on the page—-AIDS patients and those who care for them. Set in Baton Rouge, Louisiana, and written with large and frequent dollops of humor, the book is a profound meditation on faith and love in the face of illness and poverty.

Fomite
Burlington, Vermont

Kasper Planet: Comix and Tragix - Peter Schumann

The British call him Punch, the Italians, Pulchinella, the Russians, Petruchka, the Native Americans, Coyote. These are the figures we may know. But every culture that worships authority will breed a Punch-like, anti-authoritarian resister. Yin and yang—it has to happen. The Germans call him Kasper. Truth-telling and serious pranking are dangerous professions when going up against power. Bradley Manning sits naked in solitary; Julian Assange is pursued by Interpol, Obama's Department of Justice, and Amazon.com. But—in contrast to merely human faces—masks and theater can often slip through the bars. Consider our American Kaspers: Charlie Chaplin, Woody Guthrie, Abby Hoffman, the Yes Men—theater people all, utilizing various forms to seed critique. Their profiles and tactics have evolved along with those of their enemies. Who are the bad guys that call forth the Kaspers? Over the last half century, with his Bread & Puppet Theater, Peter Schumann has been tireless in naming them, excoriating them with Kasperdom....
from Marc Estrin's Foreword to Planet Kasper

Views Cost Extra - L.E. Smith

Views that inspire, that calm, or that terrify—all come at some cost to the viewer. In *Views Cost Extra* you will find a New Jersey high school preppy who wants to inhabit the "perfect" cowboy movie, a rural mailman disgusted with the residents of his town who wants to live with the penguins, an ailing screen writer who strikes a deal with Johnny Cash to reverse an old man's failures, an old man who ponders a young man's suicide attempt, a one-armed blind blues singer who wants to reunite with the car that took her arm on the assembly line—and more. These stories suggest that we must pay something to live even ordinary lives.

AlphaBetaBestiario - Antonello Borra

Animals have always understood that mankind is not fully at home in the world. Bestiaries, hoping to teach, send out warnings. This one, of course, aims at doing the same.

The Empty Notebook Interrogates Itself - Susan Thomas

The Empty Notebook began its life as a very literal metaphor for a few weeks of what the poet thought was writer's block, but was really the struggle of an eccentric persona to take over her working life. It won. And for the next three years everything she wrote came to her in the voice of the Empty Notebook, who, as the notebook began to fill itself, became rather opinionated, changed gender, alternately acted as bully and victim, had many bizarre adventures in exotic locales and developed a somewhat politically-incorrect attitude. It then began to steal the voices and forms of other poets and tried to immortalize itself in various poetry reviews. It is now thrilled to collect itself in one slim volume.

Fomite
Burlington, Vermont

My God, What Have We Done? - Susan Weiss

In a world afflicted with war, toxicity, and hunger, does what we do in our private lives really matter? Fifty years after the creation of the atomic bomb at Los Alamos, newlyweds Pauline and Clifford visit that once-secret city on their honeymoon, compelled by Pauline's fascination with Oppenheimer, the soulful scientist. The two stories emerging from this visit reverberate back and forth between the loneliness of a new mother at home in Boston and the isolation of an entire community dedicated to the development of the bomb. While Pauline struggles with unforeseen challenges of family life, Oppenheimer and his crew reckon with forces beyond all imagining.

Finally the years of frantic research on the bomb culminate in a stunning test explosion that echoes a rupture in the couple's marriage. Against the backdrop of a civilization that's out of control, Pauline begins to understand the complex, potentially explosive physics of personal relationships.

At once funny and dead serious, *My God, What Have We Done?* sifts through the ruins left by the bomb in search of a more worthy human achievement.

As It Is On Earth - Peter M. Wheelwright

Four centuries after the Reformation Pilgrims sailed up the down-flowing watersheds of New England, Taylor Thatcher, irreverent scion of a fallen family of Maine Puritans, is still caught in the turbulence.

In his errant attempts to escape from history, the young college professor is further unsettled by his growing attraction to Israeli student Miryam Bluehm as he is swept by Time through the "family thing"—from the tangled genetic and religious history of his New England parents to the redemptive birthday secret of Esther Fleur Noire Bishop, the Cajun-Passamaquoddy woman who raised him and his younger half-cousin/half-brother, Bingham.

The landscapes, rivers, and tidal estuaries of Old New England and the Mayan Yucatan are also casualties of history in Thatcher's story of Deep Time and re-discovery of family on Columbus Day at a high-stakes gambling casino, rising in resurrection over the starlit bones of a once-vanquished Pequot Indian Tribe.

Suite for Three Voices - Derek Furr

Suite for Three Voices is a dance of prose genres, teeming with intense human life in all its humor and sorrow. A son uncovers the horrors of his father's wartime experience, a hitchhiker in a muumuu guards a mysterious parcel, a young man foresees his brother's brush with death on September 11. A Victorian poetess encounters space aliens and digital archives, a runner hears the voice of a dead friend in the song of an indigo bunting, a teacher seeks wisdom from his students' errors and Neil Young. By frozen waterfalls and neglected graveyards, along highways at noon and rivers at dusk, in the sound of bluegrass, Beethoven, and Emily Dickinson, the essays and fiction in this collection offer moments of vision.

Fomite
Burlington, Vermont

Travers' Inferno - *L.E. Smith*

In the 1970's churches began to burn in Burlington, Vermont. If it were arson, no one or no reason could be found to blame. This book suggests arson, but makes no claim to historical realism. It claims, instead, to capture the dizzying 70's zeitgeist of aggressive utopian movements, distrust in authority, escapist alternative life styles, and a bewildered society of onlookers. In the tradition of John Gardner's Sunlight Dialogues, the characters of *Travers' Inferno* are colorful and damaged, sometimes comical, sometimes tragic, looking for meaning through desperate acts. Travers Jones, the protagonist, is grounded in the transcendent—philosophy, epilepsy, arson as purification—and mystified by the opposite sex, haunted by an absent father and directed by an uncle with a grudge. He is seduced by a professor's wife and chased by an endearing if ineffective sergeant of police. There are secessionist Quebecois involved in these church burns who are murdering as well as pilfering and burning. There are changing alliances, violent deaths, lovemaking, and a belligerent cat.

Still Time - *Michael Cocchiarale*

Still Time is a collection of twenty-five short and shorter stories exploring tensions that arise in a variety of contemporary relationships: a young boy must deal with the wrath of his out-of-work father; a woman runs into a man twenty years after an awkward sexual encounter; a wife, unable to conceive, imagines her own murder, as well as the reaction of her emotionally distant husband; a soon-to-be tenured English professor tries to come to terms with her husband's shocking return to the religion of his youth; an assembly line worker, married for thirty years, discovers the surprising secret life of his recently hospitalized wife. Whether a few hundred or a few thousand words, these and other stories in the collection depict characters at moments of deep crisis. Some feel powerless, overwhelmed—unable to do much to change the course of their lives. Others rise to the occasion and, for better or for worse, say or do the thing that might transform them for good. Even in stories with the most troubling of endings, there remains the possibility of redemption. For each of the characters, there is still time.

Signed Confessions - *Tom Walker*

Guilt and a desperate need to repent drive the antiheroes in Tom Walker's dark (and often darkly funny) stories:

- A gullible journalist falls for the 40-year-old stripper he profiles in a magazine.
- A faithless husband abandons his family and joins a support group for lost souls.
- A merciless prosecuting attorney grapples with the suicide of his gay son.
- An aging misanthrope must make amends to five former victims.
- An egoistic naval hero is haunted by apparitions of his dead wife and a mysterious little girl.

The seven tales in *Signed Confessions* measure how far guilty men will go to obtain a forgiveness no one can grant but themselves.

Fomite
Burlington, Vermont

The Good Muslim of Jackson Heights - *Jaysinh Birjépatil*
Jackson Heights in this book is a fictional locale with common features assembled from immigrant-friendly neighborhoods around the world where hardworking honest-to-goodness traders from the Indian subcontinent, rub shoulders with ruthless entrepreneurs, reclusive antique-dealers, homeless nobodies, merchant-princes, lawyers, doctors and IT specialists. But as Siraj and Shabnam, urbane newcomers fleeing religious persecution in their homeland discover there is no escape from the past. Weaving together the personal and the political *The Good Muslim of Jackson Heights* is an ambiguous elegy to a utopian ideal set free from all prejudice.

Meanwell - *Janice Miller Potter*
Meanwell is a twenty-four poem sequence in which a female servant searches for identity and meaning in the shadow of her mistress, poet Anne Bradstreet. Although Meanwell herself is a fiction, someone like her could easily have existed among Bradstreet's known but unnamed domestic servants. Through Meanwell's eyes, Bradstreet emerges as a human figure during The Great Migration of the 1600s, a period in which the Massachusetts Bay Colony was fraught with physical and political dangers. Through Meanwell, the feelings of women, silenced during the midwife Anne Hutchinson's fiery trial before the Puritan ministers, are finally acknowledged. In effect, the poems are about the making of an American rebel. Through her conflicted conscience, we witness Meanwell's transformation from a powerless English waif to a mythic American who ultimately chooses wilderness over the civilization she has experienced.

Short Order Frame Up - Ron Jacobs
1975. America has lost its war in Vietnam and Cambodia. Racially-tinged riots are tearing the city of Boston apart. The politics and counterculture of the 1960s is disintegrating into nothing more than sex, drugs and rock and roll. The Boston Red Sox are on one of their improbable runs toward a postseason appearance. In a suburban town in Maryland, a young couple is murdered and another young man is accused. The couple are white and the accused is black. It is up to his friends and family to prove he is innocent. This is a story of suburban ennui, race, murder and injustice. Religion and politics, liberal lawyers and racist cops. In *Short Order Frame Up*, Ron Jacobs has written a piece of crime fiction that exposes the wound that is US racism. Two cultures existing side by side and across generations--a river very few dare to cross. His characters work and live with and next to each other, often unaware of the other's real life. When the murder occurs, however, those people that care about the man charged must cross that river and meet somewhere in between in order to free him from (what is to them) an obvious miscarriage of justice.

Fomite
Burlington, Vermont

All the Sinners Saints - Ron Jacobs
A young draftee named Victor Willard goes AWOL in Germany after an altercation with a commanding officer. Porgy is an African-American GI involved with the international Black Panthers and German radicals. Victor and a female radical named Ana fall in love. They move into Ana's room in a squatted building near the US base in Frankfurt. The international campaign to free Black revolutionary Angela Davis is coming to Frankfurt. Porgy and Ana are key organizers and Victor spends his days and nights selling and smoking hashish, while becoming addicted to heroin. Police and narcotics agents are keeping tabs on them all. Politics, love, and drugs. Truths, lies, and rock and roll. *All the Sinners, Saints* is a story of people seeking redemption in a world awash in sin.

The Housing Market - Joseph D. Reich
In Joseph Reich's most recent social and cultural, contemporary satire of suburbia entitled, "The Housing market: a comfortable place to jump off the end of the world," the author addresses the absurd, postmodern elements of what it means, or for that matter not, to try and cope and function, and survive and thrive, or live and die in the repetitive and existential, futile and self-destructive, homogenized, monochromatic landscape of a brutal and bland, collective unconscious, which can spiritually result in a gradual wasting away and erosion of the senses or conflict and crisis of a desperate, disproportionate 'situational depression,' triggering and leading the narrator to feel constantly abandoned and stranded, more concretely or proverbially spoken, "the eternal stranger," where when caught between the fight or flight psychological phenomena, naturally repels him and causes him to flee and return without him even knowing it into the wild, while by sudden circumstance and coincidence discovers it surrounds the illusory-like circumference of these selfsame Monopoly board cul-de-sacs and dead ends. Most specifically, what can happen to a solitary, thoughtful, and independent thinker when being stagnated in the triangulation of a cookie-cutter, oppressive culture of a homeowner's association; A memoir all written in critical and didactic, poetic stanzas and passages, and out of desperation, when freedom and control get taken, what he is forced to do in the illusion of 'free will and volition,' something like the derivative art of a smart and ironic and social and cultural satire.

Raven or Crow - Joshua Amses
Marlowe has recently moved back home to Vermont after flunking his first term at a private college in the Midwest, when his sort of girlfriend, Eleanor, goes missing. The circumstances surrounding Eleanor's disappearance stand to reveal more about Marlowe than he is willing to allow. Rather than report her missing, he resolves to find Eleanor himself. *Raven or Crow* is the story of mistakes rooted in the ambivalence of being young and without direction.

Fomite
Burlington, Vermont

Love's Labours - Jack Pulaski

In the four stories and two novellas that comprise Love's Labors the protagonists Ben and Laura, discover in their fervid romance and long marriage their interlocking fates, and the histories that preceded their births. They also learned something of the paradox between love and all the things it brings to its beneficiaries: bliss, disaster, duty, tragedy, comedy, the grotesque, and tenderness.

Ben and Laura's story is also the particularly American tale of immigration to a new world. Laura's story begins in Puerto Rico, and Ben's lineage is Russian-Jewish. They meet in City College of New York, a place at least analogous to a melting pot. Laura struggles to rescue her brother from gang life and heroin. She is mother to her younger sister; their mother Consuelo is the financial mainstay of the family and consumed by work. Despite filial obligations, Laura aspires to be a serious painter. Ben writes, cares for and is caught up in the misadventures and surreal stories of his younger schizophrenic brother. Laura is also a story teller as powerful and enchanting as Scheherazade. Ben struggles to survive such riches, and he and Laura endure.

Four-Way Stop - Sherry Olson

If *Thank You* were the only prayer, as Meister Eckhart has suggested, it would be enough, and Sherry Olson's poetry, in her second book, *Four-Way Stop*, would be one. Radical attention, deep love, and dedication to kindness illuminate these poems and the stories she tells us, which are drawn from her own life: with family, with friends, and wherever she travels, with strangers – who to Olson, never are strangers, but kin.

Even at the difficult intersections, as in the title poem, *Four-Way Stop*, Olson experiences – and offers – hope, showing us how, *completely unsupervised*, people take turns, with *kindness waving each other on*. Olson writes, knowing that (to quote Czeslaw Milosz) *What surrounds us, here and now, is not guaranteed*. To this world, with her poems, Olson brings – and teaches – attention, generosity, compassion, and appreciative joy.
—Carol Henrikson

Entanglements - Tony Magistrale

A poet and a painter may employ different mediums to express the same snow-blown afternoon in January, but sometimes they find a way to capture the moment in such a way that their respective visions still manage to stir a reverberation, a connection. In part, that's what *Entanglements* seeks to do. Not so much for the poems and paintings to speak directly to one another, but for them to stir points of similarity.

Did you know that you can write a review on Amazon, Good Reads or Shelfari? Just go to the book page on the website and follow the links for posting a review. Books from independent presses depend on reader to reader communications.

www.ingramcontent.com/pod-product-compliance
Lightning Source LLC
Chambersburg PA
CBHW030322080526
44584CB00012B/675